GANERI, A.

Oceans

Please return or renew this item by the last date shown.
You may renew items (unless they have been requested
by another customer) by telephoning, writing to or calling
in at any library. 100% recycled paper   *BKS 1 (5/95)*

EARTH FILES

EARTH FILES – OCEANS
was produced by

David West 👥 Children's Books
7 Princeton Court
55 Felsham Road
London SW15 1AZ

Editor: James Pickering
Picture Research: Carrie Haines

First published in Great Britain in 2002 by
Heinemann Library, Halley Court, Jordan Hill,
Oxford OX2 8EJ, a division of Reed Educational and
Professional Publishing Limited.

OXFORD MELBOURNE AUCKLAND
JOHANNESBURG BLANTYRE GABORONE
IBADAN PORTSMOUTH (NH) USA CHICAGO

06 05 04 03 02
10 9 8 7 6 5 4 3 2 1

ISBN 0 431 15623 9 (HB)
ISBN 0 431 15630 1 (PB)

British Library Cataloguing in Publication Data

Ganeri, Anita
Oceans. - (Earth Files)
1. Ocean - Juvenile literature
2. Marine ecology - Juvenile literature
I. Title
551.4'6

Printed and bound in Italy

*An explanation of difficult words can be
found in the glossary on page 31.*

EARTH FILES
OCEANS

Anita Ganeri

Heinemann
LIBRARY

CONTENTS

Along the coast, where land and sea meet, the pounding force of the wind and water carve the rocks into dramatic arches, stacks and steep cliffs.

Tides, waves and currents keep the oceans in constant motion. Sometimes, an undersea volcano or earthquake triggers off a gigantic tsunami (tidal wave).

INTRODUCTION

A more accurate name for the world we live in might be Planet Ocean, not Planet Earth. Vast oceans cover two thirds of our planet, making it appear blue from outer space. The oceans are the largest habitat on Earth, home to thousands of creatures, from great white sharks and whales, to delicate sea anemones and tiny pea crabs. For human beings, the sea is a rich and vital source of food and energy. The world's highest mountains and deepest valleys all lie beneath the sea but there are still vast areas of our blue planet waiting to be explored.

Described as underwater rainforests or gardens, coral reefs teem with life. They can be hundreds of kilometres long. Yet the reefs are built by tiny sea creatures, related to jellyfish and sea anemones.

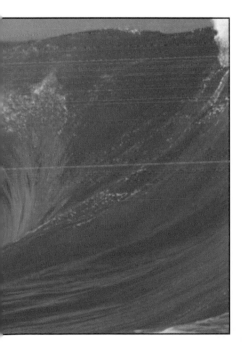

Thick feathers and a warm layer of blubber help penguins to survive along the shores of the freezing Southern Ocean.

BERING SEA

GULF OF ALASKA

NORTH AMERICA

PACIFIC OCEAN

ATLANTIC OCEAN
The Atlantic Ocean has some of the world's busiest shipping lanes and some of its richest fishing grounds.

GULF OF MEXICO

PACIFIC OCEAN
The Pacific is twice the size of the Atlantic Ocean and the biggest ocean by far. It covers about one third of the Earth.

CARIBBEAN SEA

SARGASSO SEA

Five enormous oceans cover more than two thirds of the Earth's surface. In order of size, they are the Pacific, Atlantic, Indian, Southern and Arctic. The oceans form a continuous expanse of sea, broken up by the continents.

SOUTH AMERICA

ATLANTIC OCEAN

OCEAN OR SEA?

Generally, the words 'ocean' and 'sea' are used to mean the same thing. But, strictly speaking, a sea is a smaller area of water, within an ocean, which is given a name of its own. Many seas are at least partly enclosed by land. Inland salt water lakes are also called seas.

SCOTIA SEA

WEDDELL SEA

ROSS SEA

ANTARCTICA

ARCTIC OCEAN
The smallest and shallowest ocean, the Arctic Ocean, is covered in a thick sheet of ice for most of the year.

NORTH SEA

BALTIC SEA

ASIA

SEA OF OKHOTSK

EUROPE

BLACK SEA

SEA OF JAPAN

MEDITERRANEAN SEA

PERSIAN GULF

EAST CHINA SEA

RED SEA

AFRICA

ARABIAN SEA

BAY OF BENGAL

SOUTH CHINA SEA

PHILIPPINE SEA

PACIFIC OCEAN

CELEBES SEA

JAVA SEA

BANDA SEA

INDIAN OCEAN

TIMOR SEA

CORAL SEA

AUSTRALIA

INDIAN OCEAN
Both the warmest sea (the Persian Gulf) and the saltiest sea (the Red Sea) are located in the Indian Ocean.

SOUTHERN OCEAN
The Southern Ocean surrounds the continent of Antarctica. In winter, about a third of the ocean freezes over.

SOUTHERN OCEAN

From outer space, the Earth looks blue because of all the seawater covering its surface.

7

SEAS AND SEAWATER

About 97 per cent of the world's water is salty and is found in the oceans and seas. The rest is fresh water, which is found in rivers, lakes or locked up in ice.

COLOURFUL SEAS

Not all seas look blue. A healthy sea looks green because it is full of tiny green plants, called algae. These begin the ocean food chain (see page 20). Other factors influence sea colour. The Black Sea gets its colour from the black mud it contains.

WHY IS THE SEA BLUE?

On a sunny day, the surface of the sea looks blue because it reflects blue light rays coming from the sky. Seawater deeper down also looks blue. This is because when sunlight hits the sea, blue is the last of the various colours in light to be absorbed by the water, so it reaches the furthest down.

SUNLIGHT

Blue is last to be absorbed ————

The largest sea

The Weddell Sea is part of the Southern Ocean around Antarctica. It is the world's largest sea, measuring about eight million square kilometres. For most of the year, the sea is covered in pack ice, which reaches its greatest extent during winter. It is bordered by giant ice shelves.

Main photograph: The bright, blue sea of the Indian Ocean.

SALTY SEAS

The saltiness of seawater is called its salinity. This is measured as the number of grams of salt in 1 kilogram of water, and is written as p.s.u. (practical salinity units). The average salinity of the oceans is about 35 p.s.u.

Weddell Sea, Southern Ocean.

The Red Sea gets its name from the blooms of red algae which sometimes grow on its surface. The Red Sea has the highest salinity of all seawater, at about 42 p.s.u.

WHY IS THE SEA SALTY?

Seawater is salty because of the large amounts of sodium chloride, or common salt, dissolved in it. Most of the salt comes from rocks on land, and is washed into the sea by the rain and rivers. Some comes from undersea volcanoes. Seawater also contains small quantities of other 'salts', including magnesium, calcium and sulphate.

Millions of tonnes of salt are extracted from the sea each year, in shallow salt pans along the coast.

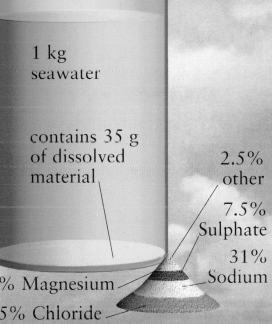

1 kg seawater contains 35 g of dissolved material

2.5% other
7.5% Sulphate
31% Sodium
4% Magnesium
55% Chloride

A remarkable landscape lies beneath the sea. Features include deep valleys, high mountains and volcanoes, huge mountain ranges and vast, flat plains, just as there are on land.

SEA FLOOR FEATURES

Continental shelf
The huge shelf of submerged land that slopes into the sea from the land. Here the sea is quite shallow.

Continental slope
The steeper slope of land extending from the continental shelf towards the deep-sea floor.

Abyssal plain
Vast, flat or gently sloping plains cover almost half the seabed.

Intertidal zone
This is the area of shoreline which is affected by the daily rise and fall of the tides.

Coastline
Along the coast, the land is battered by the force of the wind and waves.

Crust
The crust is the shell of hard rock which surrounds the Earth. It is split into pieces, called plates.

Lithosphere
The lithosphere is made up of the Earth's crust and the upper mantle.

Upper mantle
The upper mantle is a layer of partly melted rocks which lie beneath the crust.

Seamounts
Seamounts are huge, underwater mountains, usually formed by volcanic activity.

Trench
Trenches are long, narrow, V-shaped valleys in the seabed. They are created by the moving plates.

Sleds, like the one above, carry underwater cameras to photograph the seabed and collect sediment samples.

EXPLORING THE SEABED

Until recently, scientists had only a very rough idea of what the ocean floor looked like. Since the 1960s, great advances have been made in exploration technology. Today, sophisticated equipment is used to map the seabed.

CRACKING UP

The plates of the Earth's crust drift on the soft rock below, altering the shape of the seabed. Where two plates collide, one is forced under the other to form a long, narrow valley. Where two plates pull apart, molten rock rises to plug the gap. This cools and solidifies to form new ocean crust.

Spreading ridge
Ridges are mountain ranges created where molten rock rises up from the seabed, cools and hardens.

Sea spies

Satellites survey the oceans from space. They measure water temperature and wave height, as well as tracking the patterns of currents. They are also used to monitor ocean pollution and wildlife.

An ocean satellite.

GLORIA *is a long-range sonar instrument. It is towed along the seabed from a surface ship, and uses sonar (sound) to detect features, such as trenches and seamounts.*

11

Below about 1,000 metres, the sea is pitch black and freezing cold. No sunlight reaches this far down, and no plants can grow. Even so, the deep sea is home to an amazing variety of animals.

Deep-sea angler fish use their lights as bait to lure food towards their gaping mouths.

FLASHLIGHTS

Many deep-sea creatures produce their own light by chemical reactions inside their bodies. They use this light for signalling, camouflage, scaring off attackers, attracting a mate and finding food.

BLACK SMOKERS

In 1977, scientists discovered some unusual 'chimneys' deep down in the Pacific Ocean. They form where hot water, heated by volcanic activity, gushes up through cracks in the seabed. Sulphur, dissolved in the water, colours the sea black, giving these 'black smokers' their name. Giant clams and tube worms live around the chimneys.

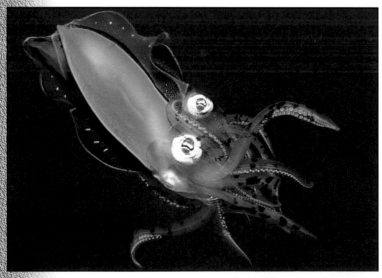

Some deep-sea squid use light for camouflage. Others squirt out luminous mucus to confuse their enemies.

These giant tube worms feed on chemicals in the hot water gushing out of the chimneys.

Some male rat-tails make a drumming sound with their bodies, to attract a mate.

Deep-sea diving

Scientists use submersibles and ROVs (remote-operated vehicles) to explore the deep sea. The deepest part of all the oceans is the Mariana Trench in the Pacific Ocean. It plummets to 10,920 metres. In 1960, the submersible, *Trieste*, dived almost to the bottom.

A modern submersible.

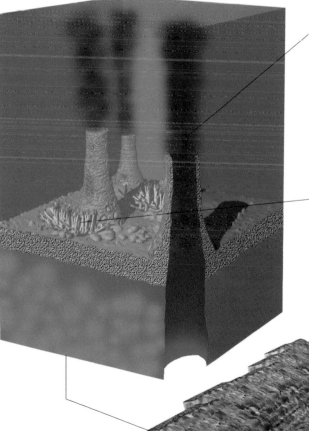

Clouds of hot, black water gush up where seawater is heated by hot, molten rocks in the ocean crust.

Clusters of giant tube worms grow around the chimneys.

Black smokers are mainly found along spreading ridges on the ocean floor.

UNDER PRESSURE

The deeper you go underwater, the greater the weight of the water pushing on you. For every 10 metres you descend, the pressure increases by one atmosphere. An atmosphere is equivalent to a 1-kilogram weight pressing on a square centimetre.

13

The water in the oceans is constantly moving. Wind blowing across the sea creates waves on the surface. The wind also drives along huge bands of water, called currents. They flow through the sea like giant rivers.

GIANT WAVES

Tsunamis are triggered by underwater earthquakes or volcanoes. These send shock waves through the water which make it bulge and ripple. In the open ocean, tsunamis are rarely more than 1 metre high but can reach speeds of over 700 km/h. As they near land, they slow down and rear up into giant waves.

The largest tsunami known was 85 metres high, almost twice as tall as the Statue of Liberty. Tsunamis can cause terrible destruction if they crash down on the shore.

El Niño

El Niño is a current of unusually warm water that sometimes appears off the South American coast. El Niño can cause chaos with the weather around the world, bringing storms, floods and tornadoes, heatwaves and drought.

Violent storm near Mexico.

WAVE MOTION

Waves look as if they are travelling forwards across the sea. In fact, waves move through the water, like ripples passing through a rope if you give it a good shake. Each water particle moves in a circle, then returns to its original place. So the water in a wave stays in the same place.

Water particles move in a circular motion.

HOT AND COLD CURRENTS

Surface currents may be as warm as 30°C or as cold as -2°C. They help to spread heat and cold around the world. They have a great effect on the weather of the places they pass by. Bergen, in Norway, enjoys quite mild winter weather because it is warmed by the Gulf Stream.

Bergen, Norway.

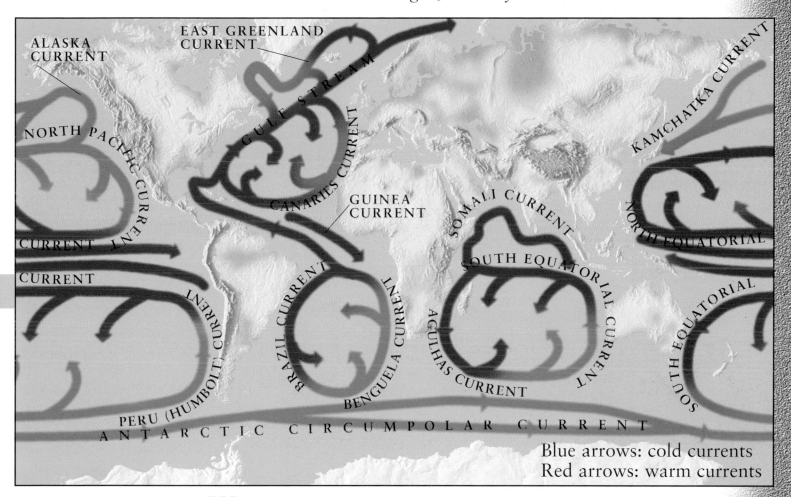

ALASKA CURRENT

EAST GREENLAND CURRENT

KAMCHATKA CURRENT

NORTH PACIFIC CURRENT

GULF STREAM

CANARIES CURRENT

GUINEA CURRENT

SOMALI CURRENT

NORTH EQUATORIAL

CURRENT

CURRENT

SOUTH EQUATORIAL CURRENT

NORTH EQUATORIAL

BRAZIL CURRENT

BENGUELA CURRENT

AGULHAS CURRENT

SOUTH EQUATORIAL

PERU (HUMBOLT) CURRENT

ANTARCTIC CIRCUMPOLAR CURRENT

Blue arrows: cold currents
Red arrows: warm currents

WORLD CURRENTS

There are two main types of currents – surface and deep water. Surface currents (shown above) are pushed along by the wind. Some of these currents are huge. The Antarctic Circumpolar Current carries about 2,000 times more water than the Amazon River. Deep water currents are set in motion by differences in water temperature and salinity.

Every day, the coastline takes a pounding from the force of the wind and waves. These smash the rocks into sand, and eat away at the cliffs along the shore.

Flowerpot rock, Bay of Fundy.

DAILY TIDES

Twice a day, the sea rises, or floods on to the shore, then ebbs, or falls away. These changes in sea level are called tides. They are mainly caused by the gravitational pull of the Moon on the Earth which makes the seawater wash back and forth.

HIGHS AND LOWS

Apart from daily tides, another tide cycle happens over 28 days. Neap tides happen when the Moon and Sun pull at right angles. This causes only a small difference between high and low tides. Spring tides happen when the Moon and Sun pull in a straight line. This causes a much bigger difference between high and low tides.

Whirlpools can form when rocks and tides block the course of an ocean current.

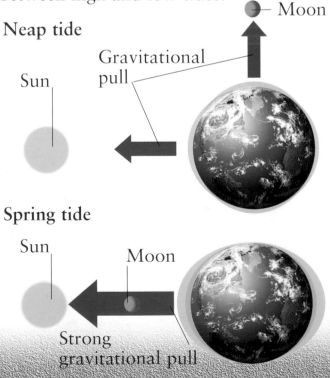

Neap tide

Moon

Gravitational pull

Sun

Spring tide

Sun

Moon

Strong gravitational pull

CARVING OUT COASTS

Along the coast, the wind and waves pound at the rocks. Rock and pebbles caught up in the waves smash into the cliffs, wearing away the shore. This process is called erosion. The bases of cliffs formed from soft rocks, such as chalk and limestone, wear away quickly. This weakens the rest of the cliff, which starts to crumble. For this reason, cliff edges are dangerous places to explore. Houses built on soft cliff tops may topple into the sea.

COASTAL FEATURES

As the wind and waves erode the rocks, they create many different coastal features. Caves on either side of a rocky headland may join up to form an arch. If the top of an arch collapses, it leaves a column of rock, called a stack.

Headland of hard rock

Cave

Cliff

Stack

Arch

Lagoon

River drops its load of silt where it meets the sea.

Salt marsh

Sand spit forms from silt deposits.

Direction of waves

Sand bar forms on gently sloping shore.

An arch and stack.

17

The Pacific is the biggest ocean, covering about 166,240,000 square kilometres. At its widest point, it stretches almost halfway around the Earth. The Pacific is also the deepest ocean.

GREAT BARRIER REEF

The Great Barrier Reef is the world's longest coral reef. It stretches for 2,028 kilometres off the north-east coast of Australia. The reef is made up of over 200 separate reefs.

The Great Barrier Reef is one of the most famous natural features of the Pacific Ocean.

In 1960, Trieste dived almost to the bottom of the 11-kilometre deep Mariana Trench in the Pacific Ocean.

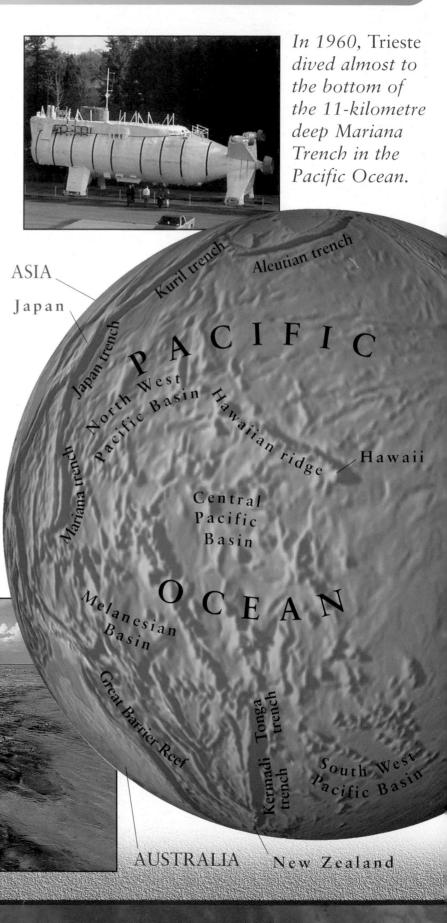

ASIA
Japan
Kuril trench
Aleutian trench
Japan trench
PACIFIC
North West Pacific Basin
Hawaiian ridge
Hawaii
Mariana trench
Central Pacific Basin
OCEAN
Melanesian Basin
Great Barrier Reef
Tonga trench
Kermadi trench
South West Pacific Basin
AUSTRALIA
New Zealand

The atoll of Bora Bora in French Polynesia, a group of islands in the South Pacific.

ISLAND LIFE

The Pacific Ocean is dotted with islands. Some are low-lying coral islands, called atolls. Atolls are coral reefs that grew on the slopes of volcanic islands. As the island sank, the coral continued to grow to form a long, narrow island around a deep, blue lagoon.

Hawaii

The tops of more than 100 underwater volcanoes make up the Hawaiian island chain. The island of Hawaii itself is formed by five volcanoes. Two of them, Mauna Loa and Kilauea, are still active. Mauna Kea, also on Hawaii, is the world's highest mountain, at 10,203 metres tall.

Hawaii.

About five million people live on the islands of the South Pacific. These dancers are from Western Samoa. The islanders depend on fish and other ocean resources for their survival.

East Pacific Rise

Peru-Chile trench

SOUTH AMERICA

Ocean plants range from microscopic algae to trailing strands of seaweed many metres long. Most ocean plants live in the top 150 metres of the sea where sunlight reaches. Plants need sunlight for photosynthesis, the process by which they make their food.

PLANT DRIFTERS

The most abundant plants in the sea are microscopic, single-celled plants, called phytoplankton. Millions upon millions of phytoplankton float near the surface of the sea. They are types of algae, the simplest kinds of plants. When plants photosynthesise (make their own food), they give out oxygen. Most of the oxygen we breathe comes from phytoplankton.

In some ocean food chains, several links in the chain are missed out. The huge basking shark feeds directly on zooplankton (inset) which it sieves from the water with its enormous, gaping mouth.

OCEAN FOOD CHAIN

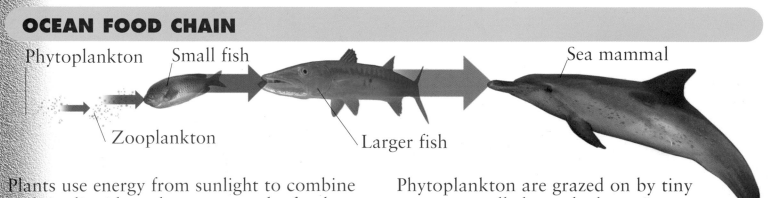

Phytoplankton   Small fish   Sea mammal

Zooplankton   Larger fish

Plants use energy from sunlight to combine carbon dioxide and water to make food. Because phytoplankton can make their own food, they start off every ocean food chain. Without them, little could live in the sea.

Phytoplankton are grazed on by tiny creatures, called zooplankton. In turn, zooplankton are eaten by fish. Bigger fish feed on the small fish, and these may be eaten by large, predatory fish or sea mammals.

The Sargasso Sea in the North Atlantic is covered in thick clumps of seaweed which float on the surface. Animals, like the Sargassum fish, mimic the weed for camouflage.

MANGROVES

Mangroves grow in muddy swamps where tropical rivers flow into the sea. Oxygen levels in the mud are low. So the trees have roots that stick up above the surface to take in air so that the trees can breathe.

Another set of roots anchors the mangrove trees in the shifting mud.

Giant seaweed

Thick forests of giant kelp seaweed grow off the Pacific coast of California, USA. Sea otters swim and feed in the kelp forests. At night, they wind strands of seaweed around their bodies to stop them drifting away in their sleep.

A kelp forest.

The oceans form the largest ecosystem for living things on Earth. They are home to a huge variety of animals, from gigantic blue whales to tiny shellfish and shrimps. These animals have adapted to moving about, communicating and finding food and a mate in the water.

Blue whale and young.

INSHORE WATERS

Rock pools
Holes in rocks fill with water as the tide comes in, providing a habitat for starfish, anemones and other creatures.

Sharks
Sharks cruise the open ocean on the look-out for prey. The most feared is the great white shark.

Crustaceans
Crustaceans include crabs, lobsters and shrimps. They live throughout the ocean, from the shore to the deep sea.

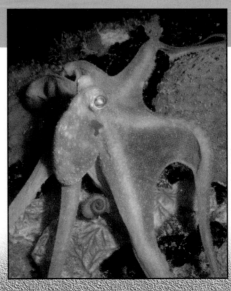

Octopus
Octopus, squid and cuttlefish are molluscs. Octopuses rest in cracks in the rocks, then swim or crawl out after prey.

Great whales

Great whales

Blue whales are the largest animals that have ever lived on Earth. They can reach a length of over 30 metres and weigh a massive 130 tonnes. A new-born blue whale weighs nearly 2 tonnes and can be over 7 metres long.

LIVING TOGETHER

Animals live in every part of the sea – in the open ocean, along the shore, on coral reefs and at every depth. Each habitat supports different animals and plants. Within their habitat, animals have to compete for space and food. Some animals work in partnership. For example, cleaner fish pick parasites off the bodies and mouths of larger fish, such as groupers. In this way, the cleaner fish get a free meal and the groupers get a thorough spring clean.

OPEN OCEAN

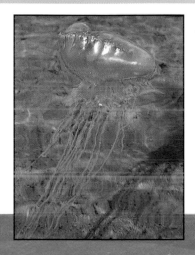

Jellyfish
Jellyfish, corals and anemones are closely related. They use their trailing, poisonous tentacles for catching food.

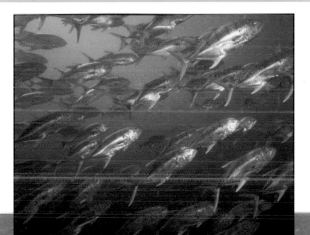

Pelagic fish
Fish, such as jacks and mackerel, live and feed near the surface of the sea. Many are caught commercially.

Sea mammals
Whales and dolphins once lived on land, but millions of years ago, their bodies adapted for life in the sea.

Squid
Squid have torpedo-shaped bodies that help them to swim fast. They move around in shoals, searching for fish.

Coral reefs are like underwater gardens, teeming with life and colour. They are home to almost a third of all the world's species of fish, together with giant clams, starfish, sea urchins and sea slugs.

WHERE CORAL GROWS

Tiny algae live inside the polyps' bodies and help to make limestone. So coral can grow in warm, shallow water where there is sunlight for the algae to make their food.

WHAT IS CORAL?

Coral reefs are formed by tiny coral polyps, related to jellyfish and sea anemones. The polyps grow hard limestone cases around their soft bodies. When they die, the cases remain and build up into a reef.

Barracuda

Grouper

Sponge

Corynactus anemones

Sergeant Major

Coral polyp

Tentacles

Mouth

Stomach

Stony base

Fairy basslet

Brain coral

Coral eater

Large chunks of the Great Barrier Reef have been eaten by crown-of-thorns starfish. To feed, a starfish forces its stomach out through its mouth and slowly digests the coral. Then it pulls its stomach back in.

Crown-of-thorns starfish.

Reef shark

Trigger fish

Garibaldi

Butterfly fish

Fire coral

LIFE ON A CORAL REEF

A coral reef is a crowded place. To avoid competition for food and shelter, life on the reef is carefully balanced between day and night. At daybreak, the reef bursts into life as day-living fish leave their hiding places to feed. At night, the reef's nocturnal residents take over, including prowling sharks.

Colourful nudibranchs, or sea slugs, live on the coral reef. Their bright colours may warn their enemies to stay away.

Coral grows in many different patterns and colours. Some corals are shaped like brains, mushrooms, feathers and antlers. The fire coral's tentacles are packed with poison but its bright yellow colouring makes it easy to avoid.

25

The Arctic and Southern Oceans lie at either end of the Earth. The polar oceans are the coldest, stormiest seas on the planet and are covered in ice for much of the year.

ARCTIC OCEAN

The Arctic Ocean is the smallest ocean. It covers about 14,000,000 square kilometres and is almost entirely surrounded by land. For most of the year, the ocean is covered in ice several metres thick.

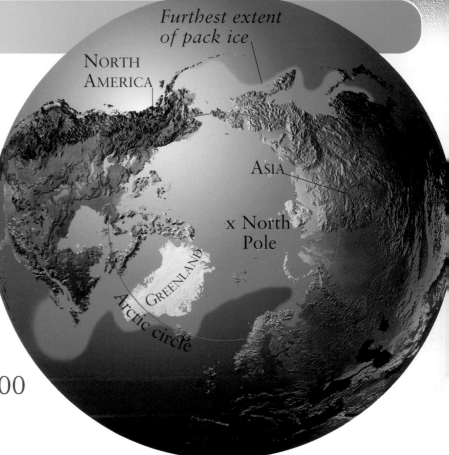

Furthest extent of pack ice

NORTH AMERICA

ASIA

x North Pole

GREENLAND

Arctic circle

Arctic
The North Pole lies in the middle of the frozen Arctic Ocean which is largely surrounded by land.

Walruses and polar bears have a thick layer of blubber under their skin to insulate them from the icy Arctic cold.

WHY ARE THE POLES COLD?

Because the Earth's surface curves, the Sun's rays strike the Poles at a wide angle. Their heat spreads out over a wide area which makes it weaker. This is why the Poles are so cold. At the Equator, the Sun's rays hit the Earth directly and are more concentrated.

Sunlight less concentrated at Pole

Sunlight more concentrated at Equator

Sunlight less concentrated at Pole

Antarctic

The South Pole lies in the middle of the frozen continent of Antarctica which is surrounded by the Southern Ocean.

SOUTH AMERICA

Furthest extent of pack ice

Antarctic circle

x South Pole

AUSTRALIA

Orcas (killer whales).

Leopard seal.

Icebergs ahead

The Arctic and Southern Oceans are littered with icebergs. These break off the ends of glaciers and ice sheets. About two thirds of an iceberg lies underwater, making them hazardous to ships. In 1912, RMS *Titanic* hit an iceberg in the North Atlantic and sank with huge loss of life.

A tabular iceberg.

SOUTHERN OCEAN

The Southern Ocean is made up of the icy seas which surround the continent of Antarctica. It is the fourth largest ocean, covering about 35,000,000 square kilometres. In winter, about a third of the Southern Ocean freezes over.

Emperor penguins.

Despite the ice and cold, the polar seas are full of food for animals such as whales, seals and penguins.

27

The oceans provide us with valuable resources, such as fish, gas and oil. But pollution is putting the seas at risk.

For divers and snorkellers, a coral reef is a thrilling underwater world.

FISHING

Each year, about 75 million tonnes of fish, such as sardine, haddock and tuna, are caught for food. In some parts of the sea, too many fish are being taken and overfishing is a serious problem.

FISHING TECHNIQUES

In some places, fishermen still use nets, hooks and spears – fishing methods that have been used for centuries. Elsewhere, fishing is big business. Traditional fishing skills are being lost as modern techniques take over. Today, many modern fishing fleets use technology, such as computers and sonar, to locate shoals of fish.

Drift nets
Drift nets hang vertically in the sea and can be many kilometres long. They drift with the tide.

Trawling
Trawl nets are dragged, or trawled, along the seabed.

Whaling
Commercial whaling is now banned because many whales are close to extinction.

Purse seining
The ends of a purse seine net are drawn together around a shoal of fish.

Traditional fishing nets in India.

TRANSPORT AND LEISURE

The oceans are vitally important for transport and trade. Merchant ships carry goods and cargo all over the world. Gigantic supertankers transport billions of barrels of oil. Ships are also used for leisure, with luxurious cruise liners taking tourists on exotic holidays.

OIL AND GAS

About a fifth of the world's oil and gas comes from the seabed. Oil was formed millions of years ago from the bodies of ancient sea creatures. Geologists survey the rocks to see if they contain oil. If oil is struck, an oil rig is built and drilling begins.

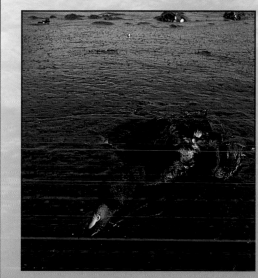

Dirty seas

All over the world, the seas are used as a dumping ground for sewage, industrial and radioactive waste and hazardous chemicals. Oil is spilt from tankers. Pollution destroys fragile habitats, such as coral reefs, and puts animals at risk.

A victim of an oil spill.

Cruise liners are like floating hotels, carrying thousands of passengers.

Hundreds of people live and work on an oil rig. Boats bring supplies from the mainland.

BIGGEST OCEAN	The Pacific is the world's biggest ocean, covering an area of 166,241,000 square kilometres which is twice the size of the Atlantic, the second largest ocean. The Pacific measures about 11,000 kilometres from north to south, and 17,700 kilometres at its widest point.
DEEPEST OCEAN	The Pacific is also the deepest of the oceans. It has an average depth of 4,200 metres but drops to 10,920 metres at its deepest point. This is at the bottom of the Mariana Trench in the north-west Pacific, the deepest point on Earth.
SMALLEST OCEAN	The Arctic is the smallest ocean and also the shallowest. It covers an area of about 14,089,600 square kilometres. It has an average depth of 1,300 metres, going down to 5,450 metres at its maximum depth. For most of the year, the Arctic Ocean is covered in ice, which is about 3 metres thick.
HIGHEST WAVE	The size of a wave depends on how fast the wind blows, how long it blows for and how far it blows. The stronger the wind, the bigger the waves. The highest wave ever recorded was 34 metres high. It was seen by the crew of the USS Ramapo in 1933.
LONGEST COASTLINE	Canada, one of the world's biggest countries, has the longest shoreline with 90,908 kilometres of coast. Indonesia is in second place. It is made up of more than 13,000 islands, spread over 8 million square kilometres of ocean, and has more than 54,000 kilometres of coast.
BIGGEST CORAL REEF	The Great Barrier Reef off the coast of north-east Australia is the biggest coral reef. It stretches for 2,028 kilometres and covers more than 200,000 square kilometres. The world's largest living structure, the Great Barrier Reef began to grow about 18 million years ago.
WORST OIL SPILL	On 24 March 1989, the oil supertanker, Exxon Valdez, ran aground in Prince William Sound, Alaska. A fifth of the ship's total cargo of oil, 43 million litres, poured into the sea. Almost 4,000 kilometres of shoreline was polluted with oil. Some 300,000 seabirds, 2,500 sea otters and millions of fish were killed.

GLOSSARY

adapted
Having special skills or features that help an animal or plant to survive in a particular place.

algae
Simple plants which range from tiny, one-celled plants to giant seaweeds.

blubber
A thick layer of fat which some animals have under their skins.

camouflage
Special colouring or markings which help to disguise an animal so that it can hide from enemies or surprise its prey.

erosion
The process by which the landscape is carved into shape by the forces of the wind, water, heat and cold.

geologists
Scientists who study the rocks of the Earth's crust.

gravitational
To do with gravity, the force which pulls two objects towards each other.

molluscs
A group of animals with soft bodies and no backbones, often protected by hard shells.

pelagic
To do with the surface of the sea.

photosynthesis
The process by which green plants use the energy in sunlight to turn carbon dioxide and water into food.

sediment
The thick layer of ooze on the bottom of a sea, lake or river.

silt
The load of sand, rocks and mud carried by rivers into the sea.

submersibles
Small submarines used for exploring the deep sea.